CHAMPIONSHIP paper planes

Flying Frog Publishing

This edition published in 1999 by Flying Frog Publishing,
107 Nob Hill Park Dr, Reisterstown, MD 21136
First published in Great Britain in 1998 by
Michael O'Mara Books Limited, 9 Lion Yard,
Tremadoc Road, London SW4 7NQ

Cover design by Chris Leishman Design
Designed by Robert Updegraff
Photography by Meg Sullivan Photography
Typeset by Florencetype Limited
Printed and bound in China

ISBN 1-884628-80-X

Contents

ADVANCED DESIGNS

UNUSUAL DESIGNS

HOW TO DESIGN YOUR OWN PLANES

Introduction

To rise above the earth and fly as free as a bird is a fantasy inside us all. Since earliest times in myth and in fact, people have tried to fly by mimicking the beating wings of a bird, but always without success. The efforts of the German glider designer Otto Lilienthal (1848–96) established the wing shape necessary to create lift on a heavier-than-air *fixed-wing* craft. Later, the American Wright brothers developed a motor-driven propeller powerful enough to keep a Lilienthal-type glider aloft, achieving the first powered flight in 1903 at Kitty Hawk, North Carolina. Their achievement was a major turning point in human history.

And yet, for all the extraordinary advances in powered flight since then, the romance of unpowered flight remains. The grace of a pencil-thin glider riding the thermals or of a hang glider descending into a valley is a sight not quickly forgotten. And the earthly equivalent of soaring silently through the air is to make, launch, and watch unpiloted gliders.

Many people make model gliders from balsa wood and tissue; many others make gliders from paper and cardboard parts cut from books and glued together for strength. But nothing can really match the pleasure of taking an ordinary sheet of paper, making a few neat folds, and then — without the aid of glue, tape, or weights — launching it with minimal effort and watching it glide smoothly through the air to a gentle landing.

The appeal of paper planes cuts across all ages and cultures, I think for several reasons. First, the speed and simplicity of the means — just simple folds in ordinary paper, nothing else. Second, the reassuringly clear way in which success or failure can be judged — either a plane flies well or it doesn't. Third, paper planes appeal to different people for different reasons — as art, science, magic, social prop, school game, creative challenge, etc. And fourth, because the graceful sight of a paper plane in flight is a temporary release from our earthly responsibilities — a moment of innocent delight and mystery. Add these reasons together, and the popularity of paper planes is easy to understand.

This book presents a collection of designs from around the world, intended to appeal both to the beginner and to the experienced enthusiast eager to make new designs. If you are new to making paper planes, please read the *Basics* chapter carefully. It will give you many useful tips on folding and flying, plus a little about the basics of origami. In addition, beginners should be wary of trying to fold the more complex designs too early — this often ends in frustration. But taking on a major challenge can sometimes be fun — you be the judge!

When folding a new design, it is most important to understand that no matter how simple a paper plane may seem, a good flier is the result of good science. Only those planes folded and flown with attention to detail will fly well. So, although the main purpose of this book is to entertain, please remember that the more care you put into the folding, the more fun you'll have from the flying.

I've had many hours of great enjoyment designing, researching, and testing the paper planes in this book. It is my sincere wish that you will have just as much pleasure from making and flying them.

Happy landings!

Paul Jackson

Why Planes Fly

Just why a *real* plane flies is a wonder of the modern age, and of course, a paper plane flies following the same principles.

This chapter describes in general terms the two *Principles of Flight*, which explain why a plane stays in the air, followed by a description of how to eliminate pitching, rolling, and yawing to achieve *Stability* in flight. You may want to skip these pages, but a basic knowledge of why a plane flies and how it can be made to fly well will greatly increase your enjoyment of making and flying paper planes, and will help correct poor flying performances.

Principles of Flight

One *"The forward thrust must be greater than the drag."*

In other words, an aerodynamic shape will enable a plane to cut efficiently through the air.

The effect of drag can be demonstrated easily with a sheet of paper. Hold it as shown so that it hangs vertically, then move your hand to the left. The entire front surface of the paper is presented to the air as the hand moves, so drag is maximized. Indeed, the bottom edge bends upward in an attempt to reduce drag.

Repeat, but now flick your wrist so that the paper is pulled horizontally through the air like a magic carpet. Notice how drag is minimized.

So, put simply, a plane will fly better if it is designed to cut through the air, rather than resist it. In other words, a paper plane should present thin edges to the air that it flies through, not flat surfaces. When seen from the front, a plane should be as invisible as possible.

However, although a minimal profile will reduce drag, a plane will not fly if the thrust is small. Thrust is provided by throwing or dropping the plane. When thrust is greater than drag, a plane will fly, though the friction of the air moving over the plane will eventually slow it to a standstill and gravity will bring it to earth.

Two *"The lift from the wings must be greater than the effect of gravity."*

Just why a wing causes a plane to lift is difficult to understand — which is why a lot of potential air passengers have a disabling fear of flying.

Put simply, if the pressure of air below the wing is greater than the pressure above it, the wing will lift. Air pressure is reduced by increasing the speed of airflow, so if the air travels faster above the wing than below it, you get lift. To achieve this, you just have to arch the top surface of the wing and flatten the bottom surface, so that the air has to travel a greater distance at a greater speed over the top surface than under the bottom one. In this way, lift is created.

This can be demonstrated by blowing down onto a strip of paper. Surprisingly, the strip *lifts*! This is because the blowing has made the air move faster across the top surface than across the bottom surface, reducing air pressure and causing the paper to lift. Try it.

Stability

A plane that adheres to the *Principles of Flight* described above may still be unstable. An unstable plane may roll, pitch, or yaw, and there are different ways to remedy each, shown here.

Roll

A plane rolls when it rotates around its lateral axis, so that as one wing dips the other rises, causing the plane to corkscrew. The way to correct this is to make a crease down the center to create a small angle between the wings, called the "dihedral" angle. Once you've added this crease, the plane will rock to and fro, but it will not corkscrew as before.

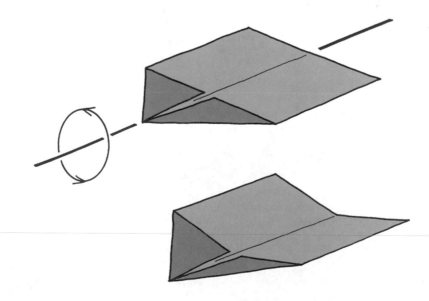

Pitch

A plane pitches when it rotates around its longitudinal axis, so that the nose rises or dips. The way to correct this is to bend the trailing corners of the wings upward for a downward dip (a nosedive) or downward for an upward rise (stalling).

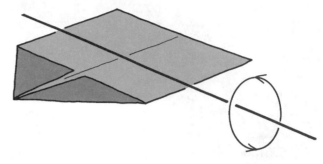

To correct a dipping nose

To correct a rising nose

Yaw

A plane yaws when it rotates around its latitudinal axis, so that it flies in circles. The way to correct this is to create a vertical surface to provide resistance against the yawing. This is usually done by creating a fuselage or rudders, or sometimes both, at the wing tips.

Fuselage

Rudders

To prevent a roll, pitch, or yaw, all three corrections are usually incorporated into the same design. A design with just one correction will not be as stable as a design with two or with all three, though some designs perform well with just one or two.

So our unstable, flat plane could be completed with a dihedral angle to prevent rolling, bent trailing wing edges to prevent pitching (nosediving or stalling), and a fuselage or rudders to prevent yawing.

Corrected plane

With the correct angle of launch and correct speed of throw — and a little trimming — it should fly well. And remember, if despite everything, your plane remains stubbornly unstable, you can always describe it as a "Stunt Special"!

Basics

Papers to Use

There is no single "best" paper for paper planes. There are, however, several types of paper which should definitely *not* be used. In particular, papers that do not hold a crease well should be avoided, including newspaper, facial tissues, and paper towels. These papers relax after being creased, ruining an aerodynamic profile.

Heavy papers of any type should also be avoided. They are simply too heavy to fly for any length of time (though you may want to experiment with them if you want to make giant planes — lighter-weight paper tends to collapse at larger scales). So avoid anything like drawing paper, pastel paper, watercolor paper, or construction paper.

In general, though, any paper about the weight of a page in this book, or a little lighter, can be used. This includes most of the inexpensive, easily available papers such as photocopy paper, typing paper, writing paper, and computer paper. If you plan to make many paper planes, it might be economical to buy thick packs of your chosen paper from a stationery store. My own preference is photocopy paper: it folds excellently, is very inexpensive, and comes in a range of attractive colors. Most small printers and walk-in photocopy shops sell a wide range of photocopy papers and also have an electric paper cutter that can cut a block of rectangular sheets into perfect squares at nominal cost, saving you a lot of work and eliminating the possibility of making those frustratingly nearly square squares!

Try using unusual papers, too. This almost endless list could include patterned wrapping paper, junk mail, paper-backed metallic foil, quality color magazine paper, thin tracing paper, lightweight handmade paper, and even disposable tablecloths. The rule here is simple: if in doubt, try it! You may be surprised at how well a plane flies when it's made from an unlikely paper — and in fact, unusual papers give any plane a "presence" that ordinary photocopy paper can never give.

Always store paper horizontally and flat, preferably away from humid or damp air. Throw away any sheets that have bent corners or crescent-shaped buckle marks, unless you know that the damaged areas will be buried deep inside the layers of the nose, where they cannot disturb the smooth flow of air over the surface of the paper.

The Best Way to Fold Paper Planes

This section may seem unnecessarily dictatorial, but I am convinced that folding paper planes demands more care than folding other types of origami models, and that some of the fine points need explanation. So, please read the following paragraphs carefully, even if you are an experienced paper folder.

Fold on a hard surface

Make *all* creases against a hard, level surface, such as a tabletop or a large hardback book. Never fold entirely in the air, on your lap, or on a soft surface such as a carpet.

Fold accurately and carefully

Paper planes will only fly well if they are folded slowly, with great attention to detail, and with great accuracy. So, at every stage, check that your folding is exactly symmetrical, that sharp points are absolutely sharp, and that delicate single-thickness wings are never accidentally bent out of shape.

Press firmly

All creases must be made firmly to help the edges cut cleanly through the air. It helps to fold smoothly and with confidence, so make your first attempt at folding a new design a dress rehearsal, not a final performance.

Smooth the layers flat

In some designs, the building up of bulky layers toward the nose and/or along the leading edge of the wings means that the paper will not lie absolutely flat against the hard folding surface beneath, but begins to bubble upward as if air is trapped inside. This bubbling increases the cross section of the plane in flight and will detract from performance.

　　The remedy is to smooth down the layers after each step. Start at the center crease and press the paper down firmly, stroking left and right toward the nose and leading edges of the wings. The crease along the leading edge will move very slightly as the paper is flattened, but this is normal.

　　Here is an example:

**Stroke the paper
outward to flatten it.**

**Stroke the paper
outward to flatten it.**

**Stroke the paper
outward to flatten it.**

Best Ways to Launch

To successfully launch a paper plane, you have to do more than just hold it in any position, with any grip, then release it with any throwing action. Every paper plane must be held and thrown in the correct way to achieve the best result. Indeed, one experienced paper plane friend of mine believes that if he only knew how to throw it, he could make a brick glide gracefully into the distance! He was joking, of course, but the point was well made.

Here then are a few general tips on holding and throwing.

Holding

Experiment throwing a plane by holding it in different places along the fuselage.

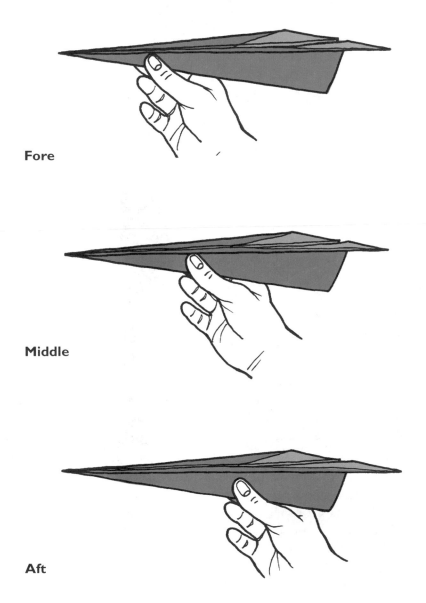

Fore

Middle

Aft

Generally, the best position is around the center of balance — the point where the plane will balance in your hand without tipping — though it is important to try other positions for comparison.

Speed

Inexperienced paper plane fliers sometimes have a tendency to throw a paper plane either too gently, so that it never catches the air and wafts sleepily to the ground, or with so much force that it careers swiftly through the air for a short distance before crashing violently. Most planes need to be launched with moderate force, though it is always worth experimenting with other speeds.

Launch angle

The four main angles of launch are vertically upward, diagonally upward, horizontal, and downward.

Vertically upward is an unpredictable launch, best executed with speed and athleticism. The intention is to hurl the plane as high as possible before it starts to level out and begin its (hopefully) slow descent. Obviously, this launch has to be done in a room with a very high ceiling, or outdoors, but success is limited. Performed well, though, this is the technique that sets world records for duration and distance, and it's worth trying just for the fun of it.

Diagonally upward at an angle between 30° and 45° is the most common and versatile launch angle. When thrown at moderate speeds, most planes will perform well. Experiment with the precise angle of launch: too steep an angle may make a plane stall, and too shallow an angle may reduce the duration or distance of the flight.

Horizontal launching creates steady, unspectacular flights and is best for delicate gliders in confined spaces. Almost all planes will fly when launched this way, but they'll probably fly better if they're launched at a different angle.

Downward launching may seem perverse, but can create excellent acrobatic flights. Try it! If the plane nosedives heavily to the ground, just curl up the trailing edges of the wings. This creates the extra lift that will bend its flight path upward. It is important always to throw with considerable speed, never gently.

"My Plane Won't Fly!"

How often I have heard this remark! The truth is that planes *rarely* fly well on a first throw. That first throw is a test to see how it performs: does it nosedive, stall, or what? Once you know what the problem is, you can try to solve it. However, it is important to remember that planes are temperamental. A plane that dives when one person throws it may stall when someone else throws it, or a plane that glides majestically into the distance on a first throw may never do it again. So, if improving the flight characteristics of a plane sometimes seems difficult, don't be discouraged — we all have the same problem.

There are, however, several reliable ways to improve a performance. By experimenting, learning from experience, and having a little luck, the ideal combination of trimming and launching can make even the most desperate no-hoper fly reasonably, even superbly.

So, before totally giving up on a plane, try these remedies.

Dihedral

This is the angle that the wings make across the top of the fuselage. Generally, a plane flies best when its wings are horizontal in flight, which means that the dihedral forms a shallow V-shape when the fuselage is pinched shut just before launching.

Dihedral when held in the hand   **The same plane in flight**

It is a common mistake to have the wings level when the plane is held in the hand, so that they point downward when the plane is in flight, like this:

Dihedral when held in the hand   **The same plane in flight**

Slightly adjusting the dihedral can dramatically affect performance. For example:

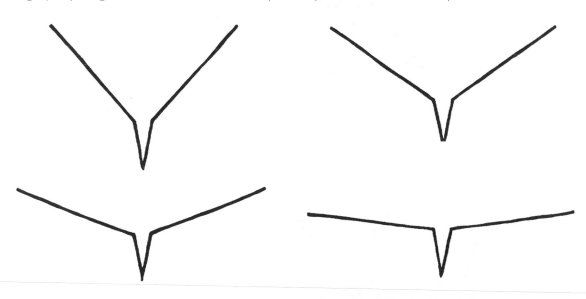

So, if your plane is not flying well, the first and simplest adjustment to make is to change the angle of dihedral.

Stalling

Stalling occurs when the plane flies upward, stops (or "stalls"), and drops like a stone. This usually happens either because the nose is too light or the back half of the plane is too heavy. In other words, the plane's center of gravity is too far back and should be moved forward.

The simplest and quickest remedy is to bend the trailing edges of the wings *downward*, like this:

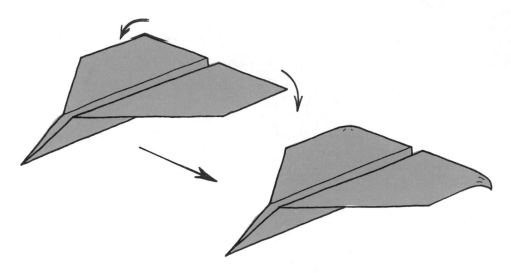

The more they are bent, the more the stalling will be compensated for, so the degree of bend is absolutely critical for a level flight. If the plane still stalls, bend more; if it nosedives, unbend a little. This simple technique is extremely effective if it is done correctly.

If no amount of bending will compensate for the stalling, try bulking up the layers at the nose by folding it back on itself once or twice, like this:

With some designs, this folding back remedy is not always possible, so instead, try adding Fun-Tack or paper clips to the nose, like this:

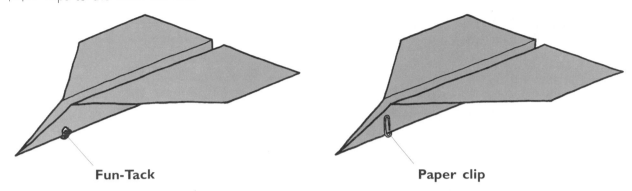

Fun-Tack   **Paper clip**

The position and exact weight of the paper clip(s) or Fun-Tack is critical, so experiment to achieve a level flight.

Nosediving

Nosediving occurs when the plane flies downward. The cause is the opposite of stalling: when a plane nosedives, either the nose is too heavy or the back half is too light, so that the center of gravity is too far forward. The only really effective remedy is to bend the trailing edges of the wings *upward*, like this:

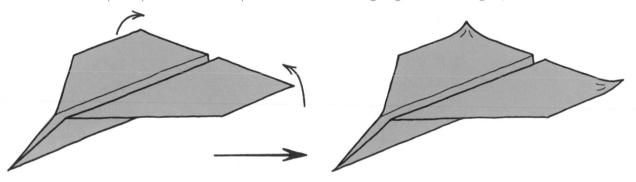

The more they are bent, the more the nosediving will be compensated for, so the degree of bend is absolutely critical for a level flight. You will probably find that *most* planes need a small upward bend of the trailing edge, regardless of design, so be prepared to do this.

Other remedies

If the remedies suggested above don't work, try these:

Holding. Experiment with holding the plane further forward or further back (see "Holding," p. 11).

Speed of launch. Experiment with faster and slower launch speeds (see "Speed," p. 12).

Angle of launch. Experiment with a higher or flatter angle of launch (see "Launch angle," p. 12).

Summary

Planes, remember, are temperamental. If your plane doesn't fly well the first time, one of the remedies suggested above should work, so go through them methodically. Sometimes the solution is a combination of remedies. You may need to increase or decrease the dihedral, *and* bend the trailing edges of the wings up or down, *and* throw your plane faster or slower than before. These experiments can all be done in seconds and with just a few test flights. Even so, finding just the right combination of remedies can sometimes be frustrating, and a newly folded plane that flew well a minute ago might not be coaxed into a repeat performance. If that happens, it's usually best to start again with a fresh sheet.

With experience, you will come to learn that a performance can rarely be predicted, but just hoped for and worked toward. Along the way, it helps to have a good sense of humor!

Symbols

The following symbols are used throughout the book to explain how the paper moves when folded.

It is important to keep looking ahead to the next step to see the results of the present step. The steps are a series of interlocking links — each one is the product of the previous step's instructions, and gives instructions to proceed to the next. So, don't look at each step in isolation, but *keep looking ahead*. Also, fold slowly and with attention to detail — be sure to follow *every* symbol on *every* step.

The symbols don't all have to be learned now, but it is important, at least, to know the difference between a valley fold and a mountain fold before you start. When you come across an unfamiliar symbol, refer back to this table.

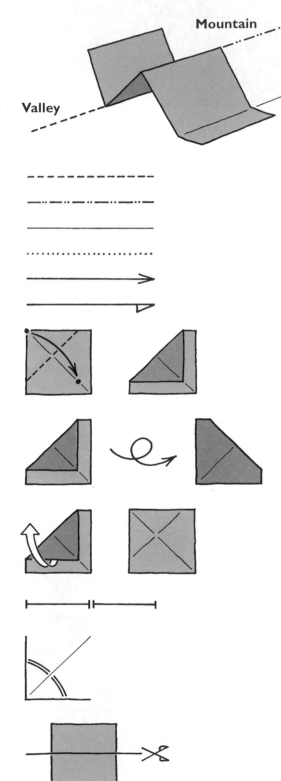

Valley	– – – – – – – – –
Mountain	—·—··—··—··—
Existing crease	————————
X-ray or projection	··························
Fold forward	⟶
Fold behind	⟹
Fold dot to dot	
Turn over	
Unfold, open out	
These distances are equal	⊢——⊣⊢——⊣
These angles are equal	
Cut	

How to Make a Square

Most store-bought paper is rectangular and needs trimming for planes that are folded from a square.

There are two methods for making a square:

1. A square with a diagonal crease

This method is suitable for planes that require a diagonal crease.

Fold over a triangle **Cut off the rectangle** **Here is the square with its diagonal crease**

2. A square without a diagonal crease

This method is suitable for planes that don't require a diagonal crease.

Carefully line up two sheets as shown, then draw a short line at the edge of the upright sheet. **Make a crease across the paper at the level of the mark.** **Cut off the rectangle.** **Here is the square without a diagonal crease.**

If only one sheet is available, the method is a little different.

Cut off a narrow edge along the bottom. The cut doesn't have to be straight. **Lay the cut piece against the rectangle and continue as above.**

How to Make a Standard "A" Rectangle

In the U.S., the most common paper sizes are letter (8½ x 11 in.), also know as American Quarto, and legal (11 x 17 in.). However, in Europe and many other parts of the world, paper is made to standard proportions and sizes are identified by "A" numbers – from A10, the smallest (26 x 37 mm, or about 1 x 1½ in.), all the way up to 4A0, the largest at 1.7 x 2.4m, or about 66 x94 in. The most common size for everyday use is A4, wich measures 210 x 297 mm, or 8³⁄₁₆ x 11¹¹⁄₁₆ in. – very close to American letter-size paper. You will see this size referred to on many of the planes in this book. The special advantage of the A4 size is that when a sheet is folded or cut in half, each half keeps the same proportions as the original sheet. This is true of every paper size in the "A" system. This amazing property, wich doesn't occur with rectangles of any other proportions, makes the standard "A" rectangle perfect for folding into paper planes.

A4 paper is very difficult to find in the U.S., but it isn't hard to convert ordinary 8½ x 11 in. letter paper into a standard "A" rectyangle. Here's how to do it:

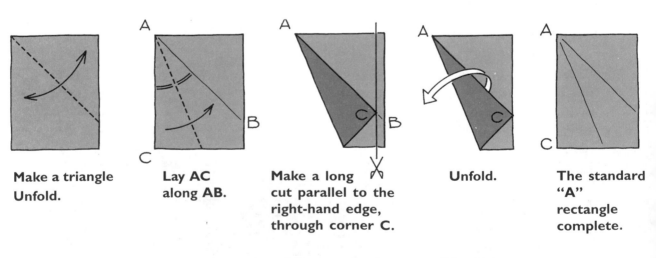

Make a triangle Unfold.

Lay AC along AB.

Make a long cut parallel to the right-hand edge, through corner C.

Unfold.

The standard "A" rectangle complete.

All the planes in the book will fly perfectly well if you make them from 8½ x 11 in. paper. However, the paper in the drawings is a standard "A" rectangle, so if you use 8½ x 11 in. paper, you may find that your planes look a little different from the drawings, and you may have to adjust a few of the folds to keep the alignments. If you want to avoid this, just convert your paper to a standard "A" rectangle as shown above.

Folding Techniques

The single crease known as the "valley fold" and its opposite, the "mountain fold," are not really techniques — they are basic folds. Techniques are established when two or more creases are handled at the same time, so that the process of folding becomes more complex.

These techniques can be grouped and named. In this book, techniques commonly known as the Squash fold, Inside Reverse fold and Outside Reverse fold are used. Rather than explain them slowly each time they occur, it is best to explain them together and just once, here in the Basics section of the book.

So, if you are unfamiliar with Squash and Reverse folds, please practice these exercises.

Squash fold

Fold in half.   **Make a diagonal crease, lifting corner A.**

Put pressure on the edge behind A, opening the pocket.   **Squash A flat and crease firmly.**

The Squash fold complete.

In the book, a Squash fold is diagramed like this:

Inside Reverse fold

Version A

Begin with Step 2 of the Squash fold, then crease and unfold as shown.

Mountain fold and unfold along the existing valley fold line.

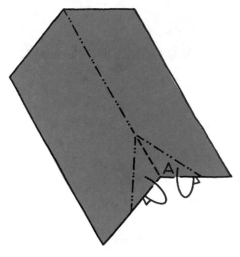

Separately crease three mountains and one valley as shown.

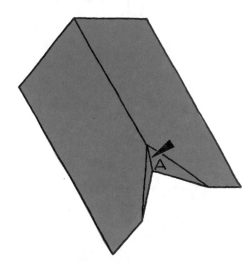

Fold the sheet in half again, but allow corner A to collapse inside between the layers, out of sight.

The Inside Reverse fold complete.

In this book, this version of the Inside Reverse fold is diagramed this way:

Version B

Fold the top edges to an existing center crease.

Fold in half.

Valley and unfold.

Mountain and unfold along the existing valley fold line.

Separately crease three mountains and one valley as shown.

Fold in half, collapsing the creases.

The Inside Reverse fold complete.

In the book, this version of the Inside Reverse fold is diagrammed like this:

Outside Reverse fold

Begin with Step 3 of Version B of the Inside Reverse fold, then valley and unfold as shown.

Mountain fold and unfold along the existing valley fold line.

Form three mountains and one valley as shown, then fold the paper in half to collapse all the creases.

The Outside Reverse fold complete.

In this book, the Outside Reverse fold is diagramed this way:

Simple Designs

The word "simple" may be misleading, because it suggests an uninteresting, basic design. In fact, a good, simple paper plane is a design of great refinement, creating an aerodynamic form with just a few folds. Also, the simple shapes of a simple design mean that such a plane will cut through the air efficiently, whereas a more complex design may create turbulence. So simple designs are usually the best fliers.

Wide Wing

Because this design is much wider than it is long, it will glide slowly through the air like a soaring bird of prey.   *Designed by Paul Jackson, U.K.*

Use A4 or 8½ x 11 in. paper.

1. Crease and unfold the shorter center crease, then bring the top corners to the crease.

2. Crease and unfold, dot to dot.

3. Fold dot to dot.

4. Again, fold dot to dot.

5

6

5. Fold over along the Step 2 crease.

6. Mountain fold the paper in half.

7

7. Create the wings, making sure that both creases are parallel to the bottom edge. The distance of the creases from the bottom edge is not critical.

8

8. The Wide Wing is complete.

Throwing Tip

Launch smoothly. If it fails to fly well, see "My Plane Won't Fly!" (p. 12) for advice.

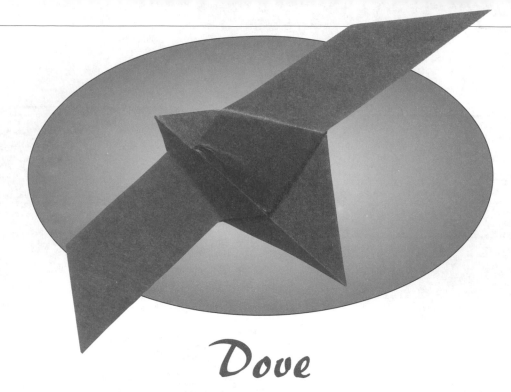

Dove

This pleasant, simple design flies superbly and with tremendous grace, though it is only barely dovelike in shape. With a little extra folding at the nose, you can create a recognizable head shape.   *Traditional Japanese.*

Use a 6–8in. (15–20cm) square of thin paper.

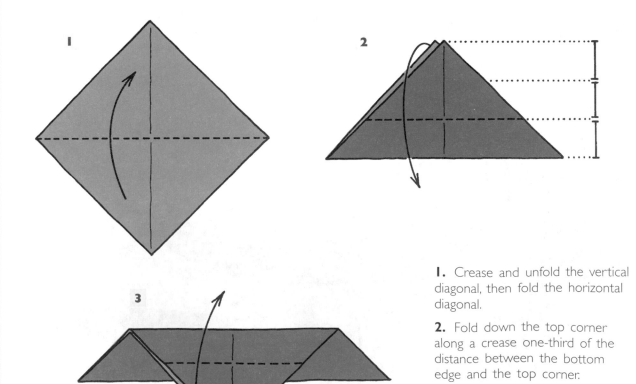

1. Crease and unfold the vertical diagonal, then fold the horizontal diagonal.

2. Fold down the top corner along a crease one-third of the distance between the bottom edge and the top corner.

3. Fold up the top layer only, along a crease placed exactly where shown.

4

5

4. Mountain fold the loose edge out of sight, tucking it as far behind as it can go.

5. Mountain fold the paper in half.

6

6. Fold the near wing down along a crease that connects where the nose triangle passes over the leading edge of the wing, and the angle where the trailing edge of the wing passes behind the tail triangle. Repeat with the other wing.

Throwing Tip

To launch, place your index finger on top of the central crease and release with a smooth flick.

7. The Dove is complete.

7

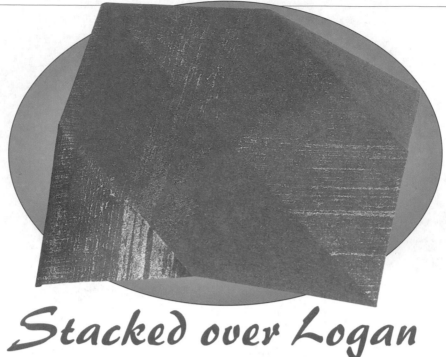

Stacked over Logan

Here is a design so simple in construction and appearance that it should not fly — but does! Its waferlike shape means that several can be stacked and launched together to create a wonderful starburst effect. *Designed by Michael LaFosse, U.S.A.*

Use a square of paper.

1. Crease and unfold both diagonals, then fold the bottom corner to the center.

2. Fold over along the diagonal.

3. Fold in the corners to the center line. Unfold.

4. Fold the bottom corners up to the top corner.

5

5. Using the Step 3 creases, tuck the loose corners into the pocket behind. This locks the paper flat.

6

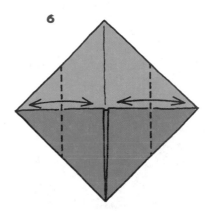

6. Fold the left and right corners to the center point. Unfold.

7

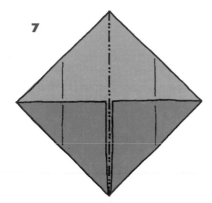

7. Mountain fold down the center.

8. Adjust the creases to this profile.

8

9. Stacked over Logan is complete.

9

Throwing Tip

To launch, place your index finger on top of the center crease and flick smoothly forward.

An entertaining variation is to make several and stack them neatly together. Launch by flicking them high into the air . . . and watch them scatter in all directions!

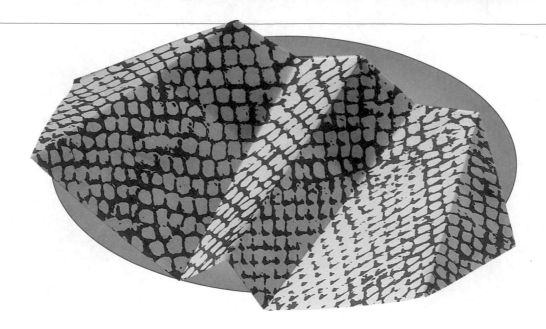

Fly Paper

Most paper planes are folded symmetrically, but this one is not. Despite the weight imbalance between the two sides of the finished design, it flies straight and true rather than around in circles, as might be supposed.   *Designed by Paul Jackson, U.K.*

Use A4 or 8¹/₂ x 11 in. paper trimmed to an "A" rectangle.

1. Crease and unfold the center crease, then bring the top left-hand corner across to the right-hand edge and crease.

2. Fold corner A across to the left.

3. Fold corner A down to the center crease.

4

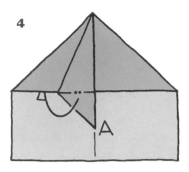

4. Tuck corner A out of sight.

5

5. Fold dot to dot.

6

6. Mountain fold the paper in half.

7

7. Fold dot to dot as shown, so that the crease is parallel to the bottom edge. Repeat behind.

8

8. Fold up a triangle as shown. Repeat behind.

9

9. The Fly Paper is complete.

Throwing Tip

Hold and launch conventionally. If it fails to fly well, see "My Plane Won't Fly!" (p. 12) for advice.

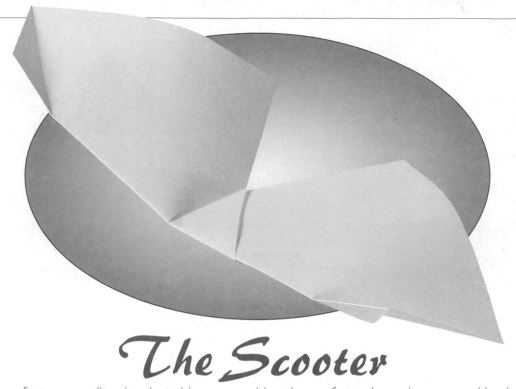

The Scooter

Few designs feature a split wing, but this one enables the craft to cleave its way recklessly through the air. Make sure you fold Step 2 accurately. *Designed by Paul Jackson, U.K.*

Use A4 or 8¹/₂ x 11 in. paper

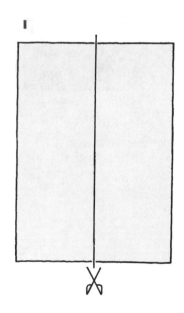

1. Cut the paper in half.

2. Fold dot to (imaginary) dot, so that triangle ABC is equilateral (all the sides are the same length).

3. Fold in half. Unfold.

4. Fold dot to dot. Unfold.

5

6

5. Again, fold dot to dot.

6. And again, dot to dot.

7

8

7. Fold over along the Step 4 crease.

8. Fold the bottom corner back.

9. Adjust the central crease to this angle of dihedral.

9

10. The Scooter is complete.

10

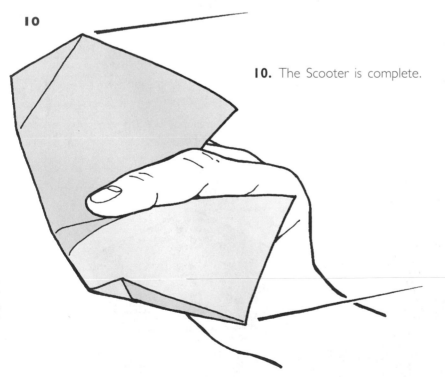

Throwing Tip

To launch, place your index finger on top of the center crease and flick smoothly forward.

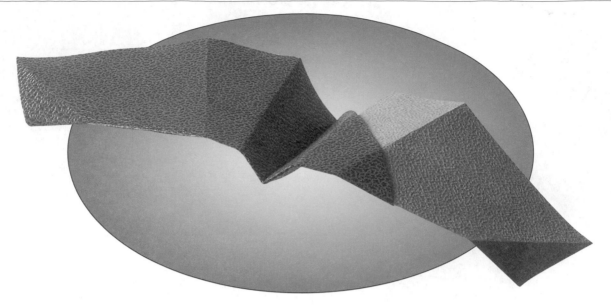

Hanging Hawk

The complex wing structure needs careful adjustment for this design to fly well, but your diligence will be well rewarded. *Designed by Stephen Weiss, U.S.A.*

Use A4 or 8¹/₂ x 11 in. paper trimmed to an "A" rectangle.

1. Trim off one-quarter of the width of the paper.

2. Turn the paper sideways, then fold the bottom left-hand corner up to the top right-hand corner.

3. Fold dot to dot as shown, making sure the crease is parallel to the bottom edge. Unfold.

4. Fold the bottom edge up to the existing crease.

5

5. Roll over along the Step 3 crease.

6

6. Mountain fold the paper in half.

7

7. Fold dot to dot. Unfold. Repeat behind.

8

8. Fold the middle pair of dots over to lie on top of the right-hand pair Unfold. Fold and unfold dot to dot at the left. Repeat everything behind.

9

9. Adjust the creases to create this profile.

10. The Hanging Hawk is complete.

10

Throwing Tip

To launch, hold the design well behind the center of gravity (if you loosened your grip, the Hawk would tip forward). If it doesn't fly well, experiment with the Step 9 profile.

Pro Glider

This bizarre craft is actually an excellent flier! Launched accurately, it will glide a considerable distance, astonishing everyone who assumes that paper fliers must be "plane" shaped.
Designed by John Smith, U.K.

Use A4 or 8½ x 11 in. paper.

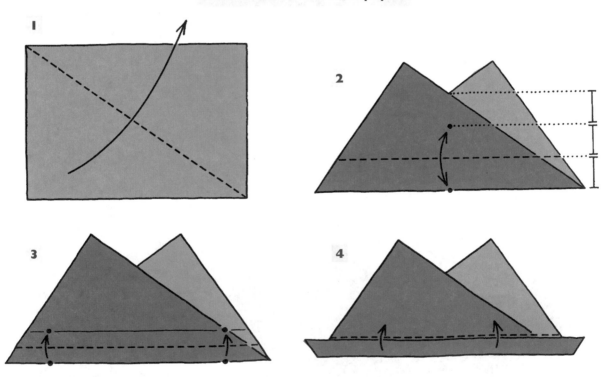

1. Crease the diagonal between the top left-hand and bottom right-hand corners. This can be awkward, so take your time.

2. Fold up the bottom edge to a point, one-third of the way between the notch and the bottom edge. Unfold.

3. Fold the bottom edge up to the Step 2 crease.

4. Fold over along the Step 2 crease.

5. Turn over.

6. Make the vertical creases as shown. Turn over.

7. With the thick band on top, roll the section between the Step 6 creases over the edge of a table. This takes a little strength, so don't be too delicate!

8. Seen from the front, this is the result. Note the straight, vertical edges flanking the curved central section.

9. The Pro Glider is complete.

Throwing Tip

To launch, put your middle finger onto the top surface of the central section and your index and ring fingers underneath to support it. Then, gently flick the Pro Glider horizontally forward. Try to do this as smoothly as possible, but not too slowly – extra speed will give a much longer flight.

Higby

The Squash fold in Step 9 creates a hollow pocket under the wing, which — unusually — does not disrupt the aerodynamic profile, but assists it. A curious and creative technique! *Designed by Stephen Weiss, U.S.A.*

Use A4 paper or 8½ x 11 in. paper trimmed to an "A" rectangle.

1. Trim off one-sixth of the width of the paper.

2. Fold in half horizontally and vertically, unfolding each crease.

3. Fold the top edge to the center.

4. Fold over along the center crease.

5. Fold in the top corners.

6. Create thin triangles as shown, tucking the center corners up inside the thick nose layers, to lock the paper flat.

7. Mountain fold the paper in half.

8. Fold down the top pair of dots to lie on top of the bottom pair. Unfold. Repeat behind.

9. Squash fold as shown (see "Folding Techniques" p. 19), creating a new crease that extends to the top right-hand corner of the paper. Repeat behind.

10. Unfold the Squash. Repeat behind.

11. Adjust the Squash fold pockets to look like the profile shown here.

12. The Higby is complete.

Throwing Tip

Hold and throw conventionally. If it doesn't fly well, see "My Plane Won't Fly!" (p. 12) for advice.

Lock-nosed Plane

Note how the Reverse fold in Step 7 and the accurately located wing crease in Step 9 lock the nose shut, so that the fuselage cannot open during flight. *Designed by Yoshihide Momotani, Japan.*

Use a 6–8 in. (15–20 cm) square of paper.

1

1. Fold a square in half, horizontally and vertically. Unfold both creases.

2

2. Fold the top edge to the center.

3

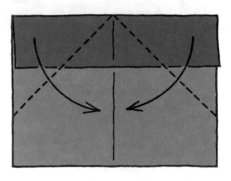

3. Fold the top corners to the center crease.

4

4. Mountain fold the paper in half.

5. Fold the nose to an imaginary point, one-quarter of the way up the vertical edge.

6. Unfold.

7. Inside Reverse fold the nose between the wings (see "Folding Techniques," p. 19).

8. Tuck the loose corner out of sight. Repeat behind.

9. Fold down the wings. Note how each crease touches the reversed nose point, and how each crease slopes gently toward the front.

10. The Lock-nosed Plane is complete.

Throwing Tip

Hold and throw conventionally. If it doesn't fly well, see "My Plane Won't Fly!" (p. 12) for advice.

Bill Glider

Remarkably simple, this reliable flier is a more elementary version of the "Hanging Hawk" (see p. 34) and the "Scooter" (see p. 32). Can you create a plane with fewer than five creases, the number used here? *Designed by Earle Oakes, U.S.A.*

Use A4 paper or a crisp dollar bill.

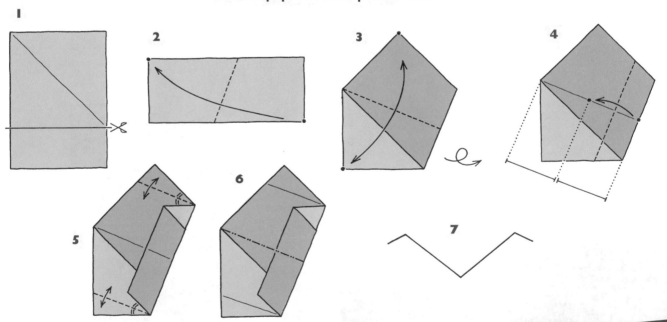

1. If you are not using a dollar bill, trim a square off an A4 or standard "A" rectangle. Keep the rectangle and discard the square.
2. Fold the bottom right-hand corner up to the top left-hand corner.
3. Fold in half dot to dot. Unfold.
4. Fold dot to dot.
5. Fold in the sides to lie against the short internal edges. Unfold.
6. Create a mountain fold down the center.
7. Adjust the creases so that the Glider has this profile.
8. The Bill Glider is complete.

Throwing Tip

To launch, place your index finger on top of the center crease, then point the Glider 45° downward and release. Don't release the Glider when it is horizontal, and don't throw it.

Advanced Designs

An advanced model is not somehow "better" than the simple ones in the preceding chapter, or more worthwhile or more clever — it is just more complicated to make. With more creases and the introduction of advanced folding techniques, many more forms are possible, and so the designs become more spectacular, adding to the entertainment value of making and flying paper planes.

Immamura Special

The shape of the Special is conventional, but the complex folding needed to create it results in an exquisitely balanced craft that glides beautifully and reliably.   *Designed by Paolo Immamura, Brazil.*

Use a 6–8 in. (15–20 cm) square of paper.

1. Crease and unfold horizontal and vertical folds. Mountain fold the top edge behind to touch the center crease.

2. Fold in the top corners.

3. Unfold everything.

4. Collapse the creases as shown to create the Step 5 shape . . .

5. . . . like this. Fold the top section on the left across to the right.

6. Fold the top layer back to the center crease.

7. Fold the top sloping edge in to the center crease.

8. Return the newly folded layers to the left.

9. Repeat Steps 5-8 with the right-hand side.

10. With mountain folds, accurately tuck the loose corners out of sight (it may be easier to crease them as valleys first).

11. Mountain fold the paper in half.

12. Create a wing crease that begins at the nose and follows the hidden thick edge of the triangle, continuing to the trailing edge of the wing. Repeat behind.

13. The Immamura Special is complete.

Throwing Tip

Hold and throw conventionally. If it doesn't fly well, see "My Plane Won't Fly!" (p. 12) for advice.

Lock Dart

The ingenious use of an Inside Reverse fold in Steps 8-10, and well-designed rudder creases in Steps 3-7, create a beautifully balanced, stable craft that is both interesting to fold and a joy to fly.   *Designed by Michael LaFosse, U.S.A.*

Use a square of paper.

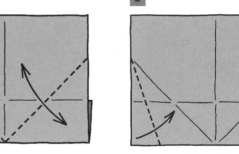

1. Crease and unfold horizontal and vertical center folds, then mountain fold the bottom edge behind to touch the center crease.

2. Fold in the bottom corners. Unfold.

3. Fold in the bottom corners to the unfolded creases, as shown.

4. Fold over along the Step 2 creases.

5. Fold dot to dot, bringing the sloping edge to lie alongside the short internal vertical edge.

6. Fold the inner dots to lie on top of the outer dots.

7. Turn over.

8. Create two valley folds on the top layer only.

9. Fold the paper in half, also folding the Step 8 creases . . .

10. . . . like this. Notice how the V-shape is collapsing inside the nose.

11. Fold down the upper dots to lie on top of the lower dots. Repeat behind. Pull open the pleated rudders.

12. The Lock Dart is complete.

Throwing Tip

To achieve the best flight performance, experiment with the rudder shapes. Hold and throw conventionally.

Chuck Finn

The bulking of the layers toward the nose up to Step 8 means that the rudders created in Step 8 will curve instead of rising straight and flat. Don't panic! The curving actually aids stability.   *Designed by Michael LaFosse, U.S.A.*

Use a 6–8 in. (15–20 cm) square of paper.

1. Crease and unfold a vertical center crease. Fold the sides to the center.

2. Fold out the loose bottom corners along diagonals, as shown. Be accurate.

3. Fold in the top corners.

4. Fold down the top point.

5. Fold down the top edge along a crease that touches what was the top point in Step 4.

6. Fold dot to dot, as shown.

7. Turn over.

8. Make vertical valley folds, as shown.

9. The Chuck Finn is complete.

Throwing Tip

To launch, place your index finger on top of the central crease and throw horizontally forward with a smooth flick.

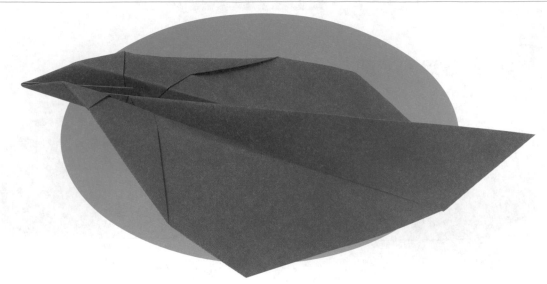

Stunt Plane

The creator is known for his Pureland designs: that is, designs made from valley/mountain folds only. The conventional way to create a tailplane is to reverse the fuselage upward, but here, the same shape is created with an ingenious Pureland pleat at Step 9. *Designed by John Smith, U.K.*

Use a 6–8 in. (15–20 cm) square of thin paper.

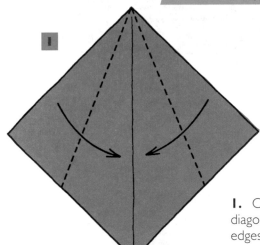

1. Crease and unfold a diagonal, then bring the top edges to the center crease.

2. Fold dot to dot.

3. Turn over.

4. Fold in the top corners.

5. Make mountain creases parallel to the center line. Note where the creases end at the top.

6. Carefully make valley creases that begin at the nose and end at the bottom of the mountains. Be accurate.

7. Now make mountain creases midway between the existing valley and mountain creases. Again, be accurate.

8. Mountain fold the paper in half.

9. To lift the wing, refold the valley and upper mountain creases. Repeat behind.

10. The Stunt Plane is complete.

Throwing Tip

Try holding, launching, and trimming it in a variety of ways to achieve long glides, loops, circular flights, and acrobatics.

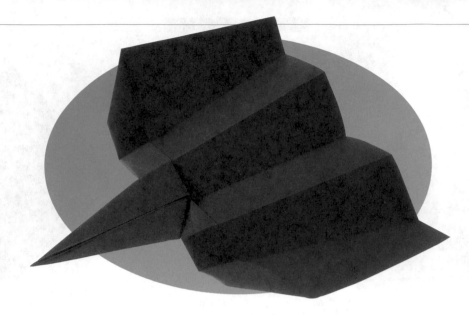

Needle Floater

The very thin nose on this design needs to be folded with great care and with some strength at Step 10. Folded well, the craft becomes an excellent flier and is an elegant sight in the air. *Designed by Nick Robinson, U.K.*

Use A4 or 8¹/₂ x 11 in. paper trimmed to a standard "A" rectangle.

1. Fold and unfold a vertical center crease. Crease quarter creases that end midway down the sheet.

2. Fold in the top corners to the quarter creases, so that both new creases begin exactly in the middle of the top edge.

3. Fold in the triangles to the center crease.

4. Fold in the sloping edges to the center, then unfold.

5. Make valley folds along the bottom edges of the thick triangles. Then make three valley folds at once, as shown, folding the nose in half and lifting it so that it points upward. Flatten the nose back down so that it points to the left.

6. Lift up corner A (the nose) and Squash fold it flat (see "Folding Techniques," p. 19).

7. Use the mountain creases made at the nose in Step 4 to swing point A upward through 180°, to create a long, thin, forward-pointing nose. Add a short horizontal valley to assist the swing, and note how the point narrows . . .

8. . . . like this. Turn over.

9. Pull down the blunt corner as far as it will go.

10. Mountain fold the paper in half.

11. The mountain fold is an existing crease. Create the valley by lowering the mountain onto the bottom edge. Repeat behind.

12. Adjust the creases so that the Floater has this profile.

13. The Needle Floater is complete.

Throwing Tip

Hold and throw conventionally. If it doesn't fly well, see "My Plane Won't Fly!" (p. 12) for advice.

The Cutter

Because of its flat, wide shape, this design will slice through the air at a surprising speed, almost as if the launch was power-assisted. *Designed by Paul Jackson, U.K.*

Use an 8 in. or (20cm) square of paper.

1. Divide a square into sixths vertically. Find the horizontal center crease and divide the top half into thirds. If you have trouble with this, divide a square into eighths, then trim off two-eighths along adjacent edges to create sixths.

2. Fold in the left and right edges along the first crease.

3. Turn in the top corners.

4. Roll the top edge back, along three mountain folds.

5. Fold out the loose corners, as shown.

6. Valley fold the paper in half.

7. Carefully fold dot to dot, creating a crease parallel to the bottom edge. Repeat behind.

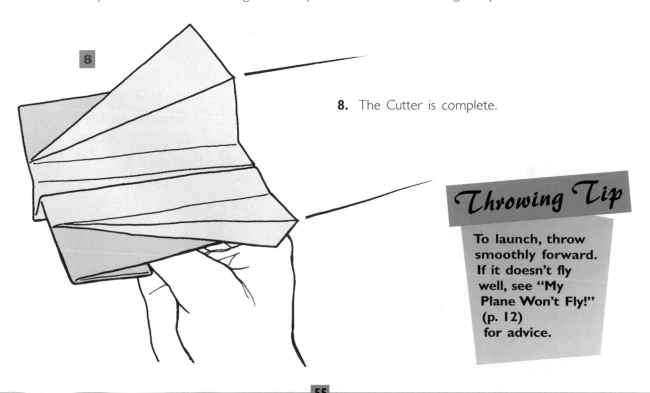

8. The Cutter is complete.

Throwing Tip

To launch, throw smoothly forward. If it doesn't fly well, see "My Plane Won't Fly!" (p. 12) for advice.

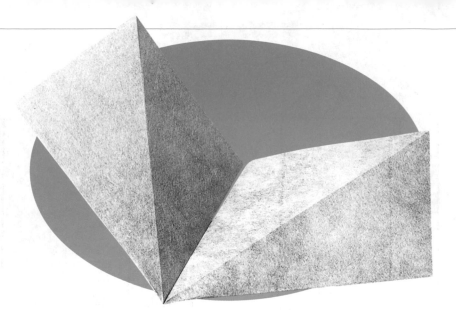

Stealth Wing

The most important step here is Step 2. Take as much time as you need to get the creases done accurately, so that Step 4 is exactly symmetrical. After that, the design still needs to be folded carefully.   *Designed by Paul Jackson, U.K.*

Use an 8 in. (20 cm) square of paper.

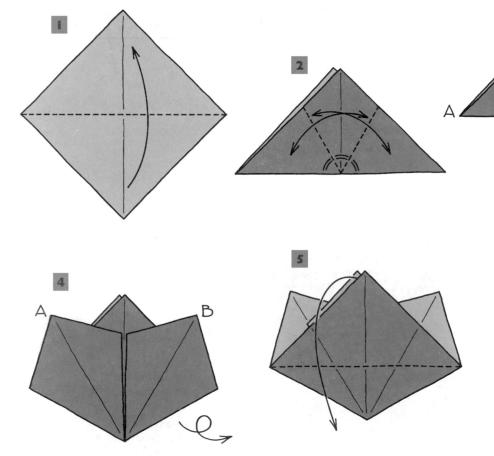

1. Crease and unfold the vertical diagonal, then fold the horizontal diagonal.

2. With two valley folds, create three equal angles, as shown. This can take a little time, so don't crease heavily until you are sure that they are accurately located. Unfold.

3. Using the valleys as guides, create Squash folds (see "Folding Techniques," p. 19). Note A & B.

4. Turn over.

5. Pull down the upper layer as far as it will go.

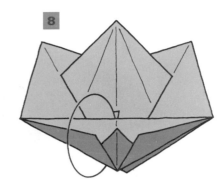

6. Fold up the bottom corner so that the crease lines up with the corner beneath. With mountain folds, narrow the top corner, then unfold.

7. Fold in the bottom corners.

8. Swing the top layer back on itself, so that it tucks neatly into the pocket behind.

9. Swing down the top corner using the mountain folds made in Step 6, adding a horizontal valley to assist the swing. Look at Step 10 to see the result.

10. Fold up the bottom point so that it does not project beyond the edges beneath.

11. Tuck the same point into the pocket beneath. No new creases are made.

12. Create a shallow mountain crease down the center. Turn over.

13. The Stealth Wing is complete.

Throwing Tip

To launch, place your Index finger on top of the center crease and throw forward with a smooth flick.

Glynn's Glider

At the time this book was written, this remarkable design held the official *Guinness Book of Records* World Record of 28.7 m (94 ft) in the Origami Distance category, set by its designer at the Yorkshire Air Museum, Yorkshire, England, on September 19, 1997. Other paper planes have flown further, but none were pure origami (folded from a rectangle without cuts and without the aid of glue, tape, weights, etc.). *Designed by Robin Glynn, U.K.*

Use A4 or 8½ x 11 in. paper trimmed to an "A" rectangle.

1

2

3

4

5

1. Crease and unfold horizontal and vertical center folds. Crease and unfold 45° diagonals on the top half, as shown. Turn over.

2. Fold dot to dot, bringing the existing mountain diagonal crease to the center point and flattening to create a new valley crease, parallel to the mountain . . .

3. . . . like this. Unfold.

4. Repeat Step 2 on the right.

5. Create vertical valleys that touch the corners of the small, creased diamond near the top edge. Be accurate.

6. Create a horizontal valley that touches the bottom corner of the same creased diamond, then a mountain, midway between the valley and the top edge.

7. Fold in the top corners. Unfold.

8. Create Squash folds (see "Folding Techniques," p. 19), swinging the single thickness top corners toward the center.

9. Fold in the top corners to lie along the Step 7 creases.

10. Refold the Step 7 creases, tucking corners A & B and corners C & D under the horizontal edge. This locks the paper flat.

11. Re-form the vertical valleys and make a central mountain crease.

13. Glynn's Glider is complete.

12. Add a rudder to the wing. Repeat behind.

Throwing Tip

Hold and throw conventionally. With only slight adjustments to the angles of the wings and rudders, it should fly a great distance.

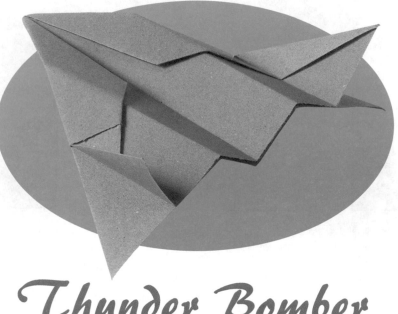

Thunder Bomber

This is one of those very pleasing designs that seems to fold itself. The sequence is somehow "obvious" and flowing, with no tricky parts. It flies superbly, too.   *Traditional.*

Use A4 or 8½ x 11 in. paper trimmed to an "A" rectangle.

1. Crease and unfold down the center, then fold the top edge down to the bottom edge.

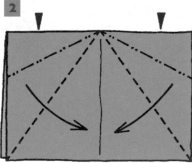

2. Create two Squash folds (see "Folding Techniques," p. 19). Note the positioning of the valley folds.

3. With mountain folds, narrow the open ends of the Squash folds.

4. Fold the Squash folds in half. The paper will then be the same, front and back.

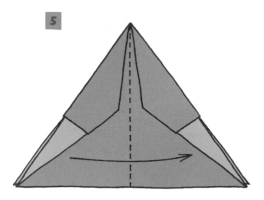

5. Valley fold the paper in half.

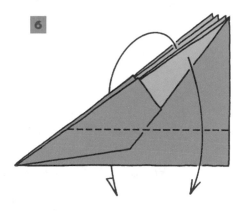

6. Valley fold the wing downward. Repeat behind.

7. Fold the top layer of the wing upward. Repeat behind.

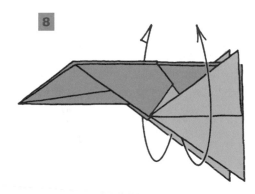

8. Lift the wings to the horizontal.

9. The Thunder Bomber is complete.

Throwing Tip

Hold and throw conventionally. If it doesn't fly well, see "My Plane Won't Fly!" (p. 12) for advice.

Classique

This design has a familiar delta shape, but carefully controlling the proportions in the Step 1 creases creates just the right amount of weight in the nose to balance the craft in flight. *Designed by Alain Georgeot and Eric Joisel, France.*

Use an 8 in. (20 cm) square of paper.

1. Fold and unfold a vertical center crease. Fold the top edge over and over, so that the lower crease is one-fifth of the way down the paper. Turn over.

2. Fold in the top corners. Unfold.

3. Fold in the sides to lie along the existing creases.

4. Fold over along the Step 2 creases.

5. Mountain fold the paper in half.

6. Fold down the wing. Repeat behind.

7. Reverse out a tailplane. Fold in the leading edge of the wing. Repeat behind.

8. Fold up the wing tip. Repeat behind.

9. The Classique is complete.

Throwing Tip

Hold and throw conventionally. If it doesn't fly well, see "My Plane Won't Fly!" (p. 12) for advice.

Launch Assist

This plane has a conventional shape, but adding the spike means it can be thrown with great force. The angle of dihedral remains the same after launch, so that the plane is immediately aerodynamic and will fly.   *Designed by Paul Jackson, U.K.*

Use a 6–8 in. (15–20 cm) square of paper.

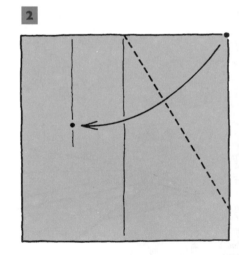

1. Crease and unfold down the center. Fold the left-hand quarter crease, but not all the way down to the bottom edge.

2. Fold the top right-hand corner across, so that it lies on the quarter crease in such a way that the new crease begins exactly in the middle of the top edge.
Be accurate.

3. Fold dot to dot. The left-hand and right-hand layers should all line up exactly.

4. Crease and unfold. Note the position of the crease.

5

5. Unfold.

6

A   C   B

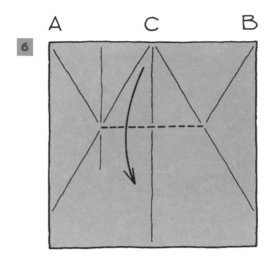

6. Crease *only* the short horizontal section shown . . .

7

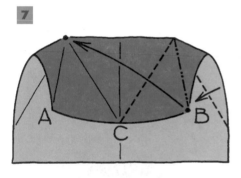

7. . . . like this. Fold corner B up to the top left corner, flattening the right-hand side of the paper.

8

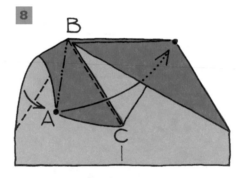

8. Repeat on the other side with A. Note how A tucks right underneath the top layer to lock the paper flat.

9

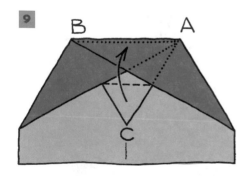

9. Fold up corner C.

10

10. The next drawing enlarges C.

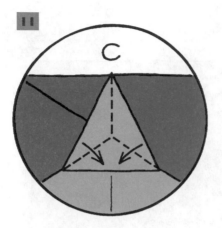

11. On the triangle below C, make three separate creases, one into each corner, then refold the lower pair.

12. This creates a 3-D spike at C. Mountain fold the paper in half.

13. Note C. Fold the upper pair of dots down to the lower pair. Repeat behind.

14. The Launch Assist is complete.

Throwing Tip

To launch, hold the spike firmly and throw high into the air. If it doesn't fly well, see "My Plane Won't Fly!" (p. 12) for advice.

Unusual Designs

"Will *that* fly?" is the way people may respond to a design that looks as un-aerodynamic as a brick, but which — magically — can still remain aloft. This chapter, then, is where you'll find the odd, the unlikely, the unexpected, and the bizarre. Included too are a few spinners, which, while not strictly planes, will often remain aloft longer than a conventional plane. So, prepare to be amazed — and enjoy.

Swan

This is one of those rare designs that seems obvious when you look at it, but which is actually very creative — would *you* have thought of it? It is little more than a very basic traditional paper dart, with an additional Reverse fold at Step 5. The result is dramatically different.   *Designed by Yoshihide Momotani, Japan.*

Use a 6–8 in. (15–20 cm) square of paper.

I. Crease and unfold down the center, then fold in the top corners.

2. Bring the sloping edges to the center crease.

3. Valley fold in half.

4. Crease and unfold the wing. Repeat behind. Note that the creases go exactly to the nose.

5. Reverse fold the nose (see "Folding Techniques," p. 19). Note that the bottom end of the crease is just in front of the midpoint of the bottom edge.

6. Refold the Step 4 creases, forming the wings and narrowing the neck.

7. Reverse fold the head. Lift up the wings.

8. The Swan is complete.

Throwing Tip

Hold and throw conventionally. If it doesn't fly well, see "My Plane Won't Fly!" (p. 12) for advice.

Butterfly

The key to folding this design successfully is in Step 1: take your time to make AB twice CD. With practice, the completed Butterfly will not only glide, but will flutter like a real butterfly.   *Designed by Paul Jackson, U.K.*

Use a 3–6 in. (7.5–15 cm) square of thin paper for a fluttering effect and larger, heavier squares for the glide.

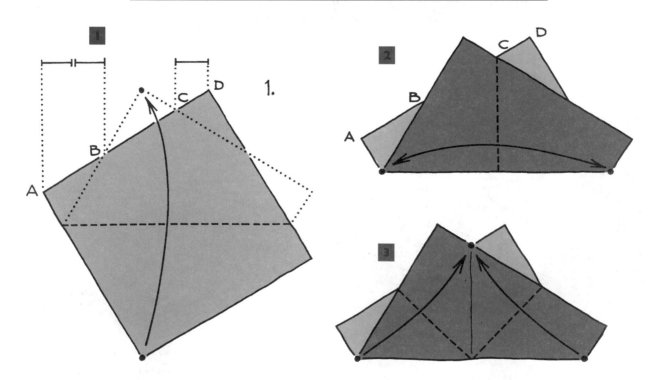

1. Fold the bottom corner up to the dotted position, in such a way that AB is twice CD. Take your time. Look at Step 2. Note that the outline of the paper will be symmetrical.

2. Fold in half, dot to dot.

3. Fold the bottom corners up to the central dot.

4. Pull down the top layer only, left and right. Look at Step 5 to see the exact shape you are trying to achieve.

5. Fold the bottom corner up to the horizontal edge, then fold up again, level with the edge.

6. Turn over.

7. Fold the loose corners inward. Create a shallow mountain crease down the center. Turn over.

9. The Butterfly is complete.

8. Adjust the creases so that the Butterfly has this profile.

Throwing Tip

To launch, place your index finger on top of the central crease and throw forward with a gentle flick.

Envelope Glider

Easier to make and easier to remember than its companion design, the Envelope Stunt Plane (see p. 74), this unusual glider is remarkably well-balanced in the air when one considers the unlikely source of the paper. *Designed by Earle Oakes, U.S.A.*

Use a smooth tea bag envelope.

1. This is the pocket side of the envelope. Note A & B. Turn over.

2. Fold the center crease. Unfold.

3. At the pocket end, fold in the corners.

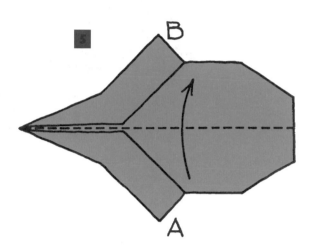

4. Narrow the nose again, but allow corners B & A to flip into view. Look at Step 5.

5. Fold in half.

6. Fold down the wing. Repeat behind. Inside Reverse fold the tailplane (see "Folding Techniques," p. 19).

7. The Envelope Glider is complete.

Throwing Tip

To launch, hold near the tail and throw smoothly forward.

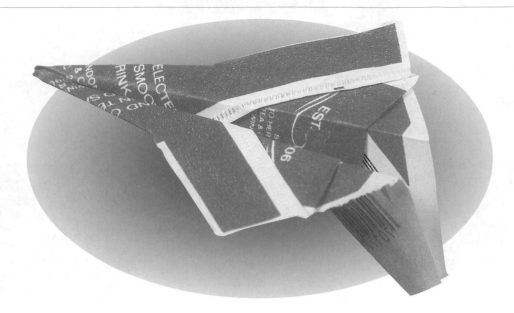

Envelope Stunt Plane

This fun design is ideal to make in a restaurant, at a party, at a meeting, or at any social occasion that needs livening up. With practice, it can be made to perform an amazingly wide repertoire of stunts.   *Designed by Earle Oakes, U.S.A.*

Use a smooth tea bag envelope.

1. This is the pocket side of the envelope. Note A & B. Turn over.

2. Fold the center crease. Unfold.

3. At the pocket end, fold in the corners.

4. Narrow the nose again, but allow corners B & A to flop into view. Look at Step 5.

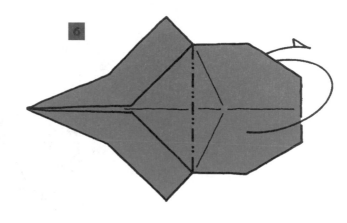

5. Fold dot to dot twice as shown, to create a shallow "V" across the center.

6. Mountain fold where shown. Unfold.

7. Carefully collapse all the creases at once until the Step 8 shape is achieved.

8. Make a wing crease that connects the tip of the nose with the rearmost corner of the plane. Repeat behind. Keep the point of the nose as neat as possible.

9. The Envelope Stunt Plane is complete. It can be held and launched in a variety of ways to achieve different stunts.

Throwing Tip

Try launching it horizontally, or holding the nose and throwing it to the side, or holding the nose and throwing it vertically with the tailplane facing you.

Bat

Designed in the early 1970s, when the creator was still a boy, the Bat is an effective variation on a well-known 2-piece plane, in which a long, narrow tail is pushed into a shape that resembles the Bat.   *Designed by David Morgan, U.K.*

Use a 6–8 in. (15–20 cm) square of thin paper.

1. Fold the bottom edge up to the top edge. Unfold. Fold the left-hand edge across to the right-hand edge. Unfold. Turn over.

2. Crease a diagonal. Unfold. Crease the other diagonal. Unfold.

3. Collapse both diagonals and the horizontal mountain . . .

4. . . . like this. Notice how B & A move down to touch C & D. Fold B & A up to E.

5. Create three creases on the left and right triangles, then collapse them . . .

6. . . . like this, on the left. The loose corner should be flattened so that it points upward, as shown on the right.

7. Turn over.

8. Fold dot to dot.

9. Outside Reverse fold the ears (see "Folding Techniques," p. 19). Valley fold the wing tips.

10. Make a shallow mountain crease down the center. Turn over.

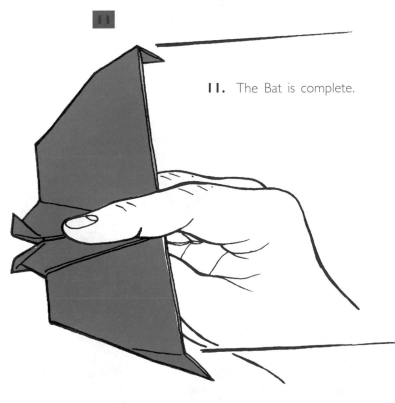

11. The Bat is complete.

Throwing Tip

To launch, place your index finger on top of the central crease and flick smoothly forward.

Human Cannonball

A design as whimsical as this one shouldn't fly at all, and it actually does take a little coaxing. The secret is to curl the trailing edges of the arms upward to just the right angle, after which our brave hero will glide a surprising distance, even without a safety net! *Designed by Jean-Jerome Casalonga, France.*

Use an 8 in. (20 cm) square of thin paper.

1. Begin with Step 4 of the Bat (see p. 76). Lift and Squash fold the front right-hand flap (see "Folding Techniques," p. 19).

2. Fold the Squash fold over to the right.

3. Repeat Step 2 on the left.

4. Repeat Step 3.

5. The paper is now symmetrical. Narrow the corners at the bottom, front layer only.

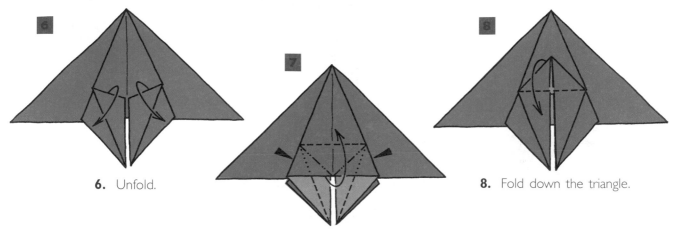

6. Unfold.

8. Fold down the triangle.

7. Lift the raw horizontal edge that crosses the middle. Allow the sides to collapse inward along the Step 5 creases. Flatten the paper to look like Step 8, swiveling the raw edge upward. Note the horizontal valley and the two mountain creases.

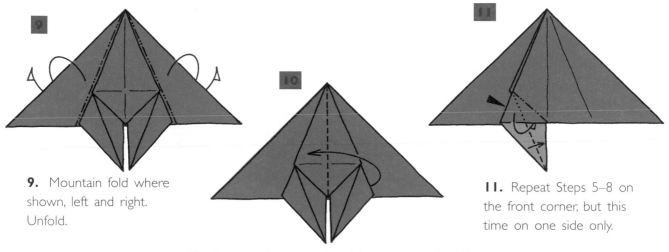

9. Mountain fold where shown, left and right. Unfold.

11. Repeat Steps 5–8 on the front corner, but this time on one side only.

10. Fold the layers on the right across to the left, but leave the big triangle at the rear in position.

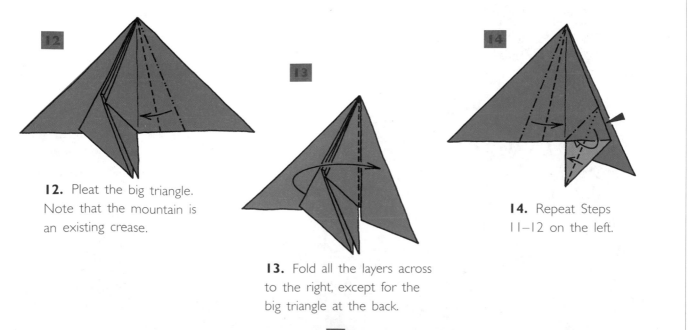

12. Pleat the big triangle. Note that the mountain is an existing crease.

14. Repeat Steps 11–12 on the left.

13. Fold all the layers across to the right, except for the big triangle at the back.

15. Fold all the remaining layers on the left across to the right.

16. Inside Reverse fold the top corner (see "Folding Techniques," p. 19). Note the exact position of the crease.

17. Pull back the arm as far as it will go. Repeat behind.

18. Reverse the feet. Pleat the face to create a nose.

19. The Human Cannonball is complete.

Throwing Tip

Curl the trailing edges of the arms upward. To launch, throw horizontally forward at moderate speed. Adjusting the angle of curl will improve the glide.

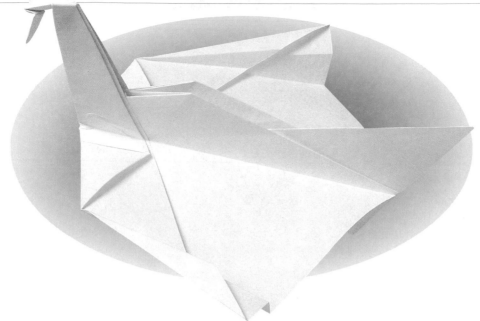

Gliding Swan

Of all the designs in the book, this one may be the least graceful, yet it flies very reliably if it's folded accurately.   *Designed by Paul Jackson, U.K.*

Use an 8 in. (20 cm) square of thin paper.

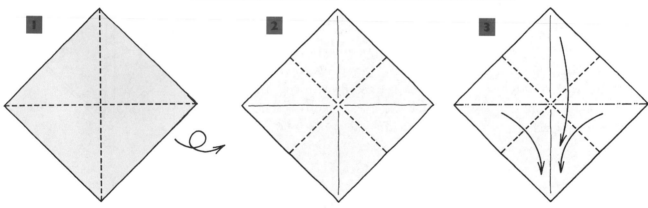

1. Crease a diagonal. Unfold. Crease the other diagonal. Unfold. Turn over.

2. Fold one edge across to the opposite edge. Unfold. Fold an adjacent edge across to the opposite edge. Unfold.

3. Collapse the two valleys and the horizontal mountain as shown.

4. Note the open corner at the bottom. Fold in the lower edges of the top flaps, left and right ...

5. ... like this. Fold down the top corner.

6. Unfold the Step 4 and Step 5 creases.

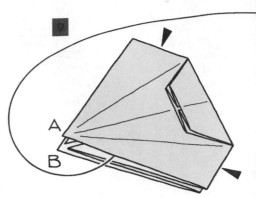

7. Crease where shown. Unfold the paper almost back to Step 3, then sink the top corner down inside the layers. This isn't easy, so take your time!

8. Refold the Step 5 crease.

9. Lift the single layers at A up into the air . . .

10. . . like this, pulling it over to the right. It will begin to fall flat, forming a narrow diamond shape . . .

11. . . like this. Notice how A has moved a considerable distance. Swing the top layer on the left and right around to the back. This is difficult and is best done by unfolding the paper to increase flexibility.

12. Fold the diamond in half.

13. Fold the left-hand section of the square around the back to the right.

14. Reverse fold out the middle poir (see "Folding Techniques," p. 19). Look at Step 15 to see its exact location.

15. Narrow the top corner. Repeat behind.

16. Fold up the near wing. Note the exact position of the crease. Repeat behind.

17. Reverse fold the head. Pleat the wing. Repeat behind. Note how the mountain crease meets the trailing edge of the wing at 90°.

18. Pleat the beak . . . **19.** . . . like this.

20. Adjust the creases until the Swan has this profile.

21. The Gliding Swan is complete.

Throwing Tip

To launch, hold just behind the point of balance and throw gracefully forward. If it doesn't fly well, see "My Plane Won't Fly!" (p. 12) for advice.

Helicopter

This spinner is unusual because it is not dropped, but thrown high into the air to begin its descent, which increases both its entertainment value and its time aloft.

Designed by Robert Abes, U.S.A.

Use a 6–8 in. (15–20 cm) square of paper.

1. Begin with Step 4 of the "Gliding Swan" (see p. 81). Rotate the paper so that the open corner is at the top. Fold down the top layer. Repeat behind.

2. Fold corner D across to lie on top of corners C and B. Fold B behind to lie behind corner A.

3. Fold A, B, C, and D to the center, so that all the creases go to the bottom point . . .

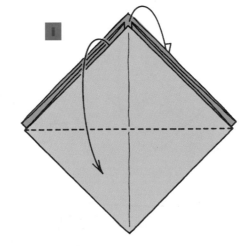

4. ... like this. Fold A across to lie on top of D. Fold C behind to lie behind B. This undoes Step 2.

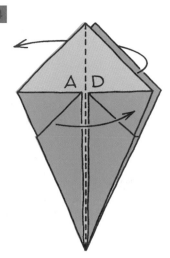

5. Fold the right-hand blade behind and the left-hand blade forward. Crease firmly.

6. The Helicopter is complete.

Throwing Tip

To launch, hold the solid point and throw as hard as possible, high into the air. The blades spin best when they form a "Y" -shape, not a "T" .

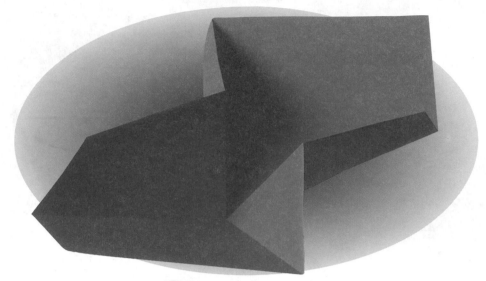

Twirly

This is easy to make, but the drawings need to be followed very carefully, because it is surprisingly easy to lose one's sense of up, down, left, and right.   *Designed by Nick Robinson, U.K.*

Use a 3–8 in. (7.5–20 cm) square of paper.

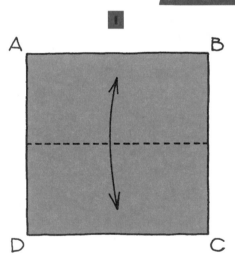

1. Fold across the center. Unfold.

2. Fold corner C up to corner A. Unfold. Turn over.

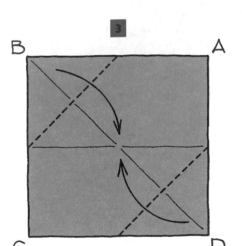

3. Fold corners B and D to the center line.

4. Fold corner C to corner A. Unfold.

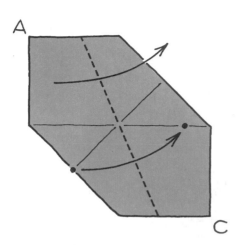

5. Fold dot to dot. Note how the new crease intersects with the others at the center point. Look at Step 6 to see the result.

6. Fold A downward.

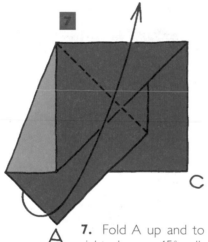

7. Fold A up and to the right along a 45° valley fold.

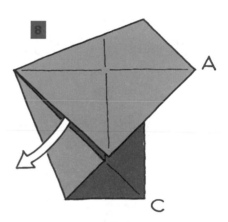

8. Pull open the layers to make a 3-D form.

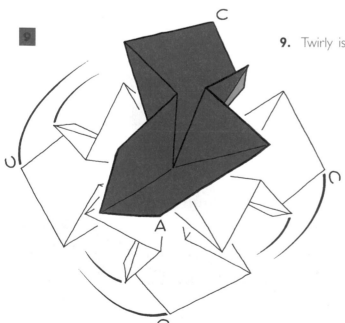

9. Twirly is complete.

Throwing Tip

To launch, hold high above your head and release, point down. As it descends, it will spin gracefully! Experiment with how open or closed the form should be to achieve the best rate of spin.

Sycamore Seed

There are many spinning sycamore seed designs, but this is the only one that can be folded from large sheets to increase the visual impact of the spin.   *Designed by John Smith, U.K.*

Use an "A" rectangle of any size, including very large ones 2–3 ft. (60–90 cm) across.

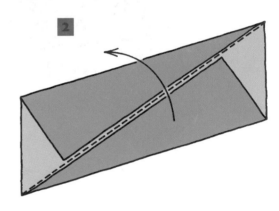

I. Begin by creasing a long diagonal. Unfold. This can be tricky, so take your time. Fold in the long edges to lie along the diagonal crease.

2. Fold in half along the existing diagonal crease.

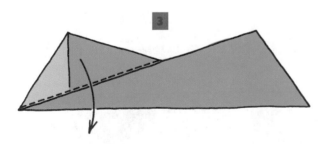

3. At the left, fold down the triangle.

4. Tuck the excess behind.

5. Fold the top edge down behind. Note where the crease ends at the bottom left.

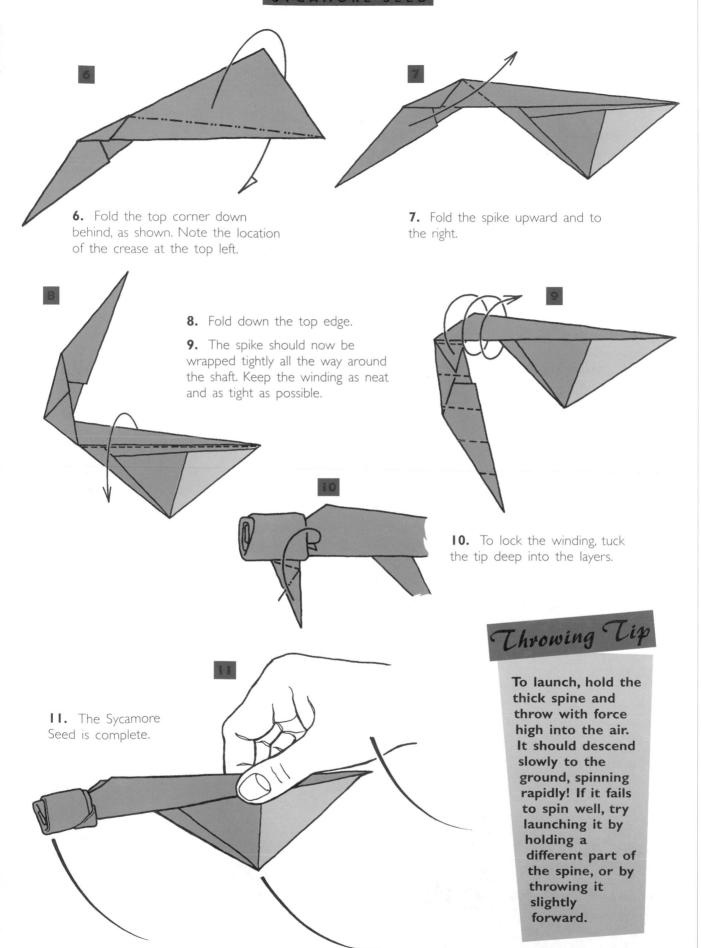

6. Fold the top corner down behind, as shown. Note the location of the crease at the top left.

7. Fold the spike upward and to the right.

8. Fold down the top edge.

9. The spike should now be wrapped tightly all the way around the shaft. Keep the winding as neat and as tight as possible.

10. To lock the winding, tuck the tip deep into the layers.

11. The Sycamore Seed is complete.

Throwing Tip

To launch, hold the thick spine and throw with force high into the air. It should descend slowly to the ground, spinning rapidly! If it fails to spin well, try launching it by holding a different part of the spine, or by throwing it slightly forward.

How to Design Your Own Planes

For the enthusiast, making and flying the planes in this book will be great fun. However, nothing can really match the thrill of designing your own plane and seeing it glide effortlessly into the blue yonder. I am convinced that designing paper planes is easier than designing for other types of origami, because a plane only has to fly — it doesn't need to *look like* a dog or a flower or whatever. Here then, is a beginner's guide.

Be motivated

First, remember that nobody achieves anything without effort. You need to *want* to design a paper plane. If you're motivated, you'll be more patient, more determined to succeed, and less defeated by any failures. If you are only prepared to try it for a few minutes and to give up forever when your first plane crashes on its very first flight, then you probably won't design a very good plane.

So ask yourself . . . are you *really* motivated?!

Format

The next step is to decide on a paper format. This is usually a simple choice between a square and a rectangle, though you may wish to experiment with strips, triangles, and other shapes.

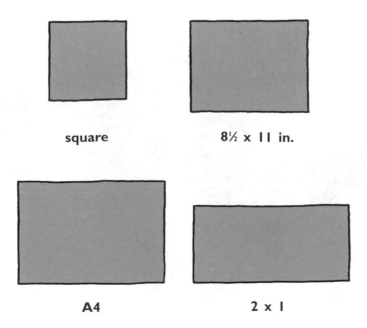

square   8½ x 11 in.

A4   2 x 1

Line of symmetry

The choice of where to place that all-important first crease, to establish the line of symmetry, is a surprisingly wide one. Here are some suggestions:

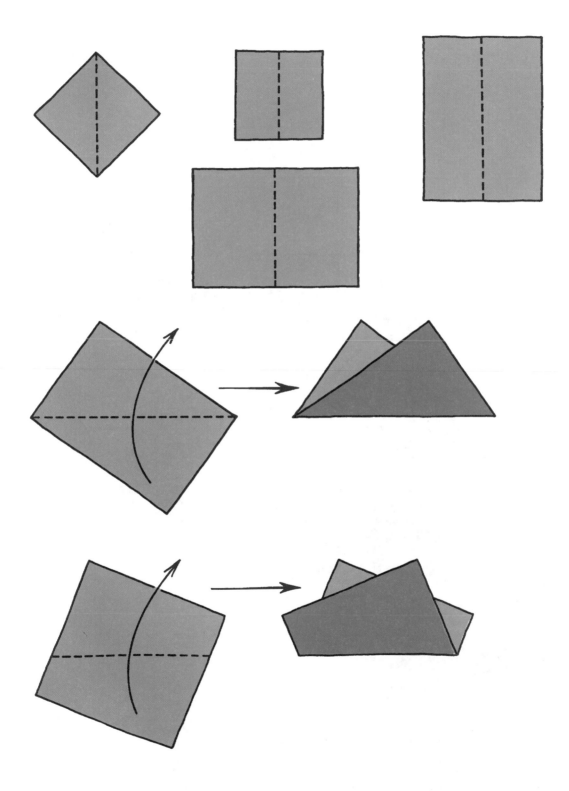

The first few folds

The first few folds are a little like the opening moves — or "gambit" — in a game of chess. There are just a few sensible first moves in chess, and the same is true when folding paper. The trick is to establish an end shape for a "folded gambit" that may not necessarily resemble a plane, but which has all the potential of becoming one (or many). Clearly, it is impossible to show all the gambits here (there probably isn't enough paper in the world), so to illustrate the point, here are a series of possible developments — or gambits — from a single opening move.

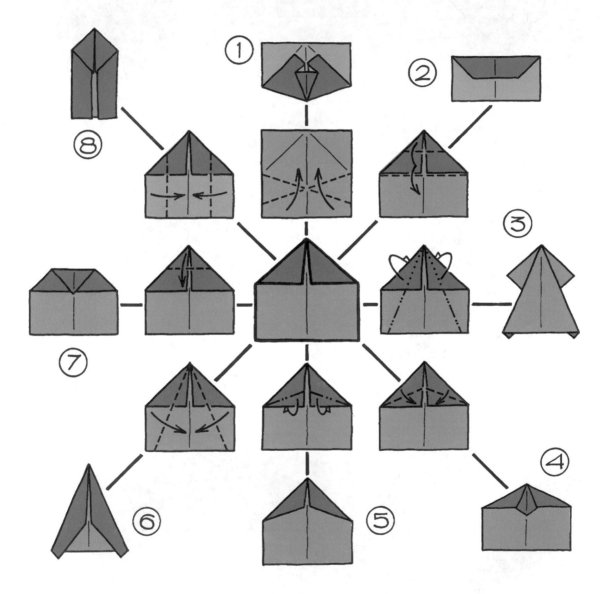

Of course, there are many other developments from the same simple shape, and many of the eight shown could be combined. Similarly, there are many other simple shapes that can be developed from one of the other creases suggested in the previous section. In other words, when you consider all the possible gambits from all the possible line of symmetry creases from all the paper formats, the number of shapes possible after just a few folds is immense.

Bulk the layers at the front

All paper planes, no matter what their design, must be heavier at the front than at the back in order to have momentum through the air. This is achieved by bulking up the layers toward the nose and thinning them out toward the tail. So when designing, remember to pull the layers forward somehow. The way you do this will be a central part of the design.

If too much paper is pulled forward, the excessive weight will make the plane nosedive; if too little is pulled forward, the craft will stall. Experimentation will tell you just how to distribute the paper to achieve a level flight. Try these variations, then combine them with the different wing shapes and trimming ideas suggested below.

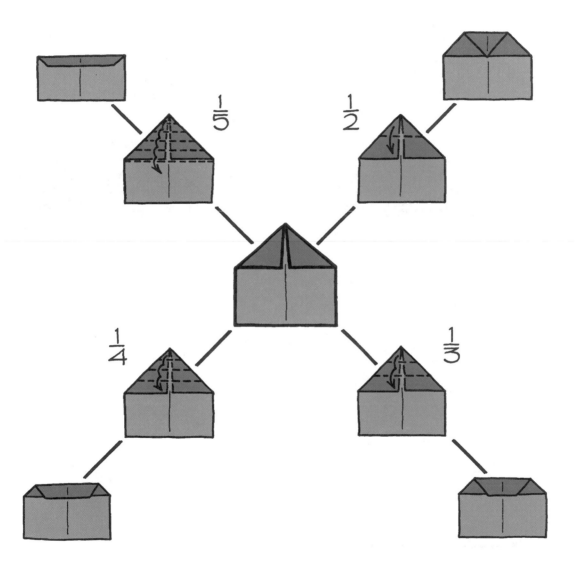

Wing shapes

The shape of the wings makes a surprising difference to the performance of a paper plane. Try these variations with a conventional paper dart to compare performances, then try them with a design of your own creation.

Sometimes, extra stability and lift can be gained by adding more creases to the wings. Try these, seen here from the front.

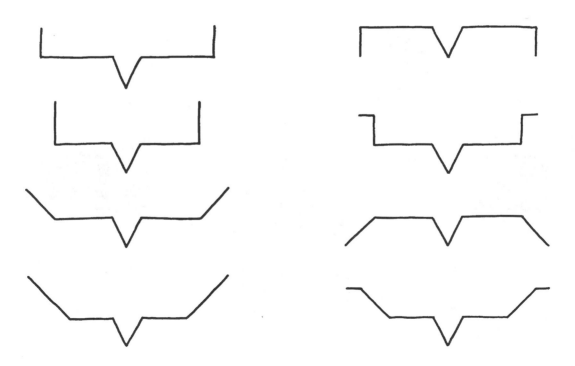

Trimming

Once you have a plane that "feels" like it should fly, it can be trimmed — that is, fiddled with until its profile and speed through the air enable it to fly as well as possible. As before, this can only be achieved with experimentation.

Before trimming a plane, launch it to see how it performs. Read the sections on "Stability" (p. 7) and "My Plane Won't Fly!" (p. 12) for suggestions on how to correct poor performance. The corrections to consider can be summarized as follows:

- rolling
- pitching
- yawing
- angle of dihedral
- stalling
- nosediving
- holding position
- speed of launch
- angle of launch

Remember to fold accurately. Also, a sheet crisscrossed with many experimental creases will never fly well, so fold a fresh version for a true indication of a plane's airworthiness.

Summary

With motivation, patience, and a little luck, you *will* succeed in designing an excellent paper plane. If you need a little inspiration, look at some of the designs in this book. You might try combining ideas from different planes or deliberately trying to do the opposite of what is suggested — the results might surprise you! There is no substitute for experience, so with time your designing will become more graceful and more accurate.

If you're not sure you can design, just give it a try — you have nothing to lose except a few sheets of paper, and the rewards of seeing something that *you* have created flying gracefully from *your* hand are unbeatable.

Acknowledgments

The author would like to thank those Origami Designers who graciously gave permission for their work to be included in this book. Grateful thanks too to Earle Oakes for his magnificent illustrations and for his enthusiasm for the project.

All the designs in this book remain the copyright of the named creator and may not be folded for commercial gain without the written permission of the creator.

Any duplication of previously published designs is entirely coincidental and unintentional.

Contributors:

U.K. — Robin Glynn, David Morgan, Nick Robinson, and John Smith.
U.S.A. — Robert Abes, Michael LaFosse, Earle Oakes, and Stephen Weiss.
France — Jean-Jerome, Casalonga, Alain Georgeot, and Eric Joisel.
Brazil — Paolo Immamura.
Japan — Yoshihide Momotani.

Origami Societies

Both of these long-established, friendly organizations have a lot to offer the general origami enthusiast. Membership is inexpensive and worldwide.

British Origami Society
2a The Chestnuts
Countesthorpe
Leicester LE8 5TL
U.K.

Origami U.S.A.
15 West 77th Street
New York,
NY 10024–5192
U.S.A.